Discovering the "Titanic"

THE GREAT ADVENTURES SERIES

Discovering the "Titanic"

Jonathan Rawlinson

Rourke Enterprises, Inc.
Vero Beach, Florida 32964

Key to the successful exploration of the
Titanic, the deep submersible Alvin is
prepared for descent.

LIBRARY OF CONGRESS
Library of Congress Cataloging-in-Publication Data

Rawlinson, Jonathan, 1944-
    Discovering the Titanic/by Jonathan Rawlinson.

    p. cm. — (Great adventure series)
    Includes index.
    Summary: Describes the search for and discovery of the wrecked Titanic some seventy years after the great liner sank after hitting an iceberg.
    ISBN 0-86592-873-8
    1. Titanic (Steamship) — Juvenile literature.
2. Shipwrecks — North Atlantic Ocean — Juvenile literature. 3. Underwater exploration—North Atlantic Ocean — Juvenile literature. [1 Titanic (Steamship) 2. Shipwrecks — North Atlantic Ocean. 3. Underwater exploration — North Atlantic Ocean.]
I. Title.   II. Series.
G530.T6R38 1988   88-11115
363.1'23'091631 - dc19   CIP
                    AC

CONTENTS

The Search

It was summer 1985 when a small ship sailed out of St. Pierre, a French island south of Newfoundland. It had come from Brest, France, to begin a great search. The ship was called *Le Suroit* and it belonged to the French Institute for Research and Exploration of the Sea. Dr. Robert Ballard arrived at St. Pierre from sea tests off the Pacific coast of Mexico. He boarded the ship before it sailed on one of the greatest sea adventures of all time.

The French scientists and three American scientists led by Dr. Ballard were searching for the wreck of what was once the world's biggest ship. The *Titanic* sank on its first voyage across the Atlantic Ocean in April 1912. Now, a joint expedition between French and United States scientists was going out to find it. Would they be lucky? Only time would tell.

The French ship *Le Suroit* was quite small and very compact. There was barely enough room on board for the 50 people and extensive scientific equipment needed for the search. Included in

Research Vessel Knorr on a survey in the Antarctic during 1984, pictured here by R.D. Bowen of the Woods Hole Oceanographic Institute.

Vital to finding Titanic was Argo, seen here on the deck lab 3 habitat.

this equipment was a sophisticated **sonar** system. Getting sufficient space to work in was a real problem. It was like living on a floating college dormitory.

Sonar is a means of finding objects by studying echoes of sound waves. The equipment sends out a sound signal and records the echo. The exact nature of the echo tells scientists what has caused the reflection. Sonar is used by surface ships to detect submarines. It is also used by scientists to map the bottom of the sea. Reflected sound waves would help Dr. Ballard and the French scientists discover the giant liner far below the waves, assuming it still rested on the surface of the seabed.

Some people thought massive mudslides caused by enormous earthquakes under the sea floor would have covered the *Titanic*. Others believed it would have broken up as it sank more than two miles to the seabed. If it had broken up, the separate pieces of wreckage could have buried themselves in the silt. Nobody knew what to expect.

7

The plan had been for *Le Suroit* to search for the wreckage and for Dr. Ballard's ship the *Knorr* to send cameras down to take pictures. The French ship would locate the liner, and the American ship would come along and explore what remained on the sea floor. The *Knorr* was operated by scientists from the Woods Hole Oceanographic Institute. One of two famous sea and ocean research institutes in the United States, Woods Hole is partially funded by contracts from the government. The Office of Naval Research had given Woods Hole money to develop underwater robots that could take cameras and men far below the surface of the sea.

Throughout July, the French research ship cruised up and down across the area where the *Titanic* went down. Nobody knew the exact spot, and each person had a different idea about precisely where to look. The sonar search came to nothing, and soon the weather would turn foul. The second phase of the search involved the *Knorr*. Using cameras on underwater robots, Ballard's people hoped to have better luck. In August 1985, with high hopes of finding something, Ballard's team sailed for the area where the *Titanic* sank.

Robert Ballard hoped to find the Titanic and explore it using the Deep Submergence Vessel Alvin.

Robert Ballard explains Titanic search strategy to Martin Bowen (left center) and Navy Personnel.

Titanic: The Great Liner

By any measure, the *Titanic* was big. It was designed that way. It was owned by a large shipping company called the White Star Line. The company's biggest competitor was Cunard, and they operated fast passenger liners carrying people from Europe to America at the end of the nineteenth century. There were no aircraft, and the only means of travel across the sea was by boat. The White Star Line ships were built for comfort rather than speed. To be competitive, they decided to build a new class of ship using the latest engines. This, they thought, would give passengers comfortable rooms and a fast trip across the Atlantic.

To build the new class of passenger liner, the White Star Line chose Harland & Wolff. They would assemble these giant liners at their shipyard in Belfast, Ireland. This was the great age of shipbuilding. Between 1882 and 1912, the workforce increased from 150 to almost 15,000. Three great liners were built between 1910 and 1916. They were the *Olympic*, the *Titanic*, and the *Gigantic*. The last one, *Gigantic*, was re-named *Britannic* after the *Titanic* sank with great loss of life.

The keel for the *Titanic* was laid in March 1909. It was enormous, and the liner took two years to get ready for launch. *Titanic* had a **displacement** of 66,000 tons and a length of 882 feet.

Almost complete but with a lot of equipment still remaining to be installed, the Titanic is launched into the waters at Belfast, Ireland.

The Titanic was designed and built to provide a level of luxury unseen before in a great ocean liner.

It had three **screws** and could reach a top speed of about 25 knots (29 MPH). The *Titanic* had a crew of just over 800 people and could carry 2,230 passengers in three classes: first class, second class and third class. First-class passengers were on the top deck, and third-class passengers were at the bottom. This reflected how people thought of themselves in society at the turn of the century.

The builders put four extra lifeboats on the *Titanic* above and beyond the sixteen that were required by law. Even so, there were only enough boats for 1,178 people out of the 3,000 on board. Harland & Wolff expected to have to put thirty-two lifeboats on the *Titanic* and designed it to accommodate them. Expected changes in the law did not happen, so they only provided twenty lifeboats. Not many people believed a ship as big and well built as the *Titanic* would sink. Inside it had fifteen **bulkheads**, which were giant steel walls. If the ship hit something and was holed, only one watertight compartment would be flooded. At least, that was the idea.

Thousands of people worked on the *Titanic.* Setting records for workmanship and quality, the builders spent a lot of money to produce what was considered the best ship ever launched. Riveters worked night and day, carpenters built decks and cabins, plumbers put in thousands of toilets and wash basins, and furnishers gave it a lavish look. When it was launched in May 1911, more than 100,00 people watched it slip into the water. It was a magnificent sight, and everyone shouted and clapped with pride.

For a long time people had been booking their passage for the *Titanic's* first voyage. First-class passengers got luxury rooms, and there were two suites, each 50 feet long. Second-class passengers shared elevators, and there was a gymnasium, a Turkish bath, a swimming pool, and several restaurants. The liner was the last word in luxury. Ballrooms, bars, and smoking rooms made it one of the most comfortable ships afloat. It even had one of the new radio sets. With this, passengers could send cable messages to their friends and family. Or, in the unlikely event of a disaster, the *Titanic* could call for help.

Equipped with every luxury its passengers would need, the Titanic also had a fully equipped gymnasium.

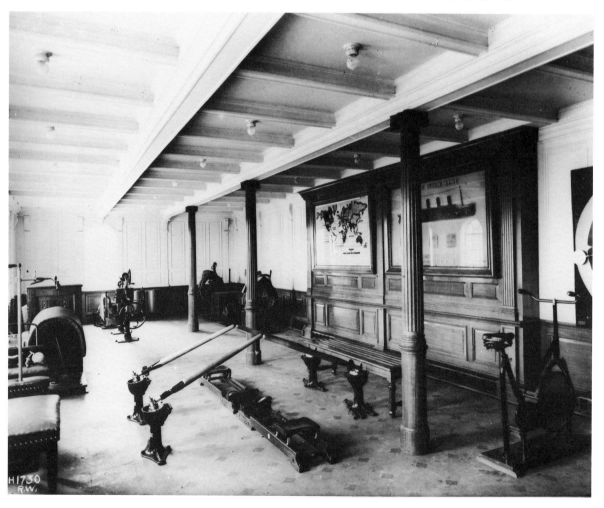

Large tugs slowly push Titanic toward its berth as the giant liner prepares for its maiden voyage across the Atlantic.

Giant machinery built to push Titanic across the Atlantic at record speed broke records in its day for size and capability.

Iceberg!

There were some extremely wealthy and well-known people aboard the *Titanic* on its first voyage. Wealthiest of all was Colonel John Jacob Astor, the great-grandson of a famous fur trader and owner of a hotel chain. Mr. Isidor Strauss, the owner of Macy's department store, and his wife were on board. Also on the *Titanic* was Major Archibald Butt, President Taft's military aide. In addition to these well-known people were bankers, steel barons, brewers, and lawyers. Among the British on board were Sir Cosmo and Lady Duff Gordon. He was a peer of the British Empire and she was a well-known dress designer with shops in Paris and New York.

The *Titanic* left Belfast for her first point of departure on the evening of April 2, 1912, arriving at Southampton docks just after midnight on the morning of April 4. Southampton is a famous seaport 78 miles southwest of London, England. There, the *Titanic* was finally loaded with stores for the Atlantic crossing, including

Cutting a dashing profile in the water, Titanic was easily distinguished by its four great funnels.

4,400 tons of coal. With the stocks already on board, the coal brought the total load to more than 6,300 tons. About 400 tons of coal was used by the boilers to make steam and operate cargo-loading winches!

Titanic sailed from Southampton at midday on April 10, the day after Easter monday. During the morning, boat trains had arrived with hundreds of first and second-class passengers. Third-class passengers made their own way to the giant liner. The *Titanic* went first to Cherbourg, France, to pick up more passengers and then called in at Queenstown, Ircland for 1,385 mail bags and still more passengers. When she finally got under way for the Atlantic crossing at 1:30 P.M. on April 11, 1912, the *Titanic* carried approximately 2,227 passengers and crew. The exact number is unknown because all known lists vary.

The great liner made good time for two days, although shortly after dawn on Sunday, April 14, *Titanic* picked up a radio message warning of ice ahead. Just before noon, a Dutch liner called on her

radio to say there was "much ice" about. Throughout the day more messages poured in, and shortly after 6:00 P.M. the temperature plummeted to 33 degrees. More messages about ice continued throughout the evening, and the *Titanic's* captain, Edward J. Smith, retired to bed at 9:20 P.M. with orders to wake him "if at all doubtful." Ironically, the 62-year-old Captain Smith was to have retired after taking *Titanic* on her maiden voyage.

It was about 11:40 P.M. when lookout man Fred Fleet saw a dark shape looming out of the crisp freezing night. Instinctively, he sounded a warning bell and telephoned the bridge. "Iceberg right ahead!" On the bridge, First Officer Murdoch ordered the ship "hard-a-starboard," but seconds later a shuddering vibration ran the full length of the ship. It was just a glancing blow, but it was enough to open the ship's plates and send water cascading into the forward boiler room. On deck, several tons of ice fell onto the liner as the iceberg drifted past and disappeared into the night. It had done its worst. The liner was doomed.

Most passengers and crew never felt or heard the impact. Within twenty minutes, however, Captain Smith knew his ship was sinking. On board was Thomas Andrews, the chief designer, and a quick survey showed the forward boiler rooms were filling up one by one. Dragging the ship down at the nose, the level of water was rising to the top of one bulkhead and spilling over to the next one behind.

Distress signals were sent out immediately, and within forty-five minutes of the collision, women and children were ordered to the lifeboats. There were not enough lifeboats for everyone. The men would have to stay behind. On deck, a band played ragtime while more than ten miles away another ship, the *Californian*, watched distress rockets from the *Titanic* soar into the sky. Thinking the passengers to be having a party, they ignored them.

As boats were lowered, most of them only half full, the passengers still could not believe the great liner was actually

Orphans from the Titanic picked up by rescue ships gather in New York.

sinking. Reality began to overwhelm them, and panic broke out as passengers scrambled for the boats. By 1:40 A.M. most of the boats were gone, and more than 1,500 people were still on board. They moved farther and farther toward the **stern** as the **bow** went underwater. There were acts of bravery and acts of great love. Mrs. Ida Strauss had been offered a seat in a lifeboat and refused. Turning to her husband, she told him, "We have been living together for many years. Where you go, I go." They sat down in deck chairs and waited.

The *Titanic* finally disappeared beneath the calm water at about 2:20 A.M. With a great roar and the sound of rolling thunder, the ship broke in two and the stern rose sharply into the sky. Minutes later, it too slid beneath the water. In all, 1,513 people were drowned, and only 714 were saved. Most of those saved were rescued by ships that picked them up from the small lifeboats. For those rescued it was indeed a night to remember.

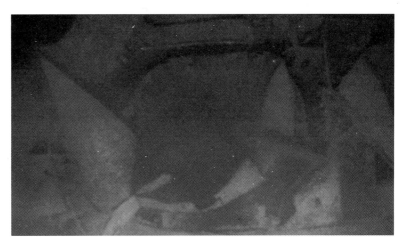

As the ship went down, the giant funnels were torn away by the water pressing down upon the giant liner. This gaping hole is all that remains of where once a large funnel was attached.

Anchor chains and windlass on Titanic's bow have remained intact for more than 70 years as the giant liner lay two miles beneath the cold waters of the Atlantic.

Ballard's Dream

Dr. Robert Ballard had always wanted to find the *Titanic*. As an ensign in the U.S. Navy and a young scientist, he arrived at Woods Hole in 1967. There he learned to dive, and he worked on the development of **submersibles**, small undersea robots capable of taking cameras or scientists far beneath the sea. The first submersible he worked on was named Alvin. It could dive to a depth of 6,000 feet, just over one mile down. That was not nearly enough for Ballard. He wanted to reach the *Titanic* more than two miles down!

In 1973, Alvin's hull was made stronger, and with this improvement he could descend more than 13,000 feet, greater than the distance needed to reach the doomed liner. But science came first, and adventure would have to wait. Few people were interested in providing the money to go after the *Titanic*, so Ballard worked on several research projects. All the while he hoped he could one day convince somebody to support the venture.

During the 1970s, Ballard made many dives, descending 20,000 feet to investigate the ocean floor and explore strange life forms. Then in 1980, Ballard received support from the Office of Naval Research. They wanted Ballard to help develop underwater equipment, and there was no better way to test it than by pulling off a spectacular demonstration. Ballard had the idea already in mind. Why not look for the *Titanic*, find it, take pictures of it, and prove how good the equipment really was? The Navy agreed.

The Research Vessel Atlantis II travels to the search site carrying Alvin in a cage on the stern.

Overleaf:

Alvin was carried in a cage at the back of the Research Vessel Atlantis II. Once free it was under the full control of its crew.

Titanic Is Found

It took several years to develop the right equipment, and much work was done before Ballard and the Navy could try it out in the cold waters of the western Atlantic. In August 1985, they were well on their way. As part of a joint expedition with French scientists, there was a good chance they would locate the great liner. The French failed to find it using sonar. Now Ballard's people would try with cameras mounted to a special cage.

Called Argo, the device would be towed below the ship from which it had been lowered. Forward-looking sonar in the bow of the ship would map the sea floor looking for objects that might be part of the *Titanic.* Cameras on Argo would take pictures of what the sonar picked up. Another robot, Angus, could also be used. Angus had its own sonar as well as special cameras. Together, the

Angus was very important for gathering information essential for finding Titanic and did much to carry out preliminary exploration of the seabed.

Debris litters a section of the hull of Titanic's stern, peeled outward by the force of the great ship's destruction some 400 miles southeast of Newfoundland.

two systems were a great step toward making underwater exploration a major scientific activity.

Just as there had been three Americans, including Ballard, on the French ship *Le Suroit* when it went hunting for the *Titanic* using sonar alone, so there were three Frenchmen on the *Knorr* with Ballard's team. Back and forth the search continued as the days rolled by. Soon the weather would bring a halt to activity for that year. The Atlantic is a turbulent place, and for only a few months in summer are conditions right for dangling robots 13,000 feet below the waves.

Argo began the first search on August 25. For several days it was lowered to 13,000 feet to search previous sonar recordings from the French team. Nothing. On August 28, Argo spun out of control and crashed into the seabed, digging itself in like an anchor.

For a few hours it looked like the expedition would lose its star performer. Then Argo pulled free, and the search continued. After several days, the boredom was finally broken.

It was a few minutes to one on the morning of September 1, 1985, when the cameras on Argo transmitted the first pictures of

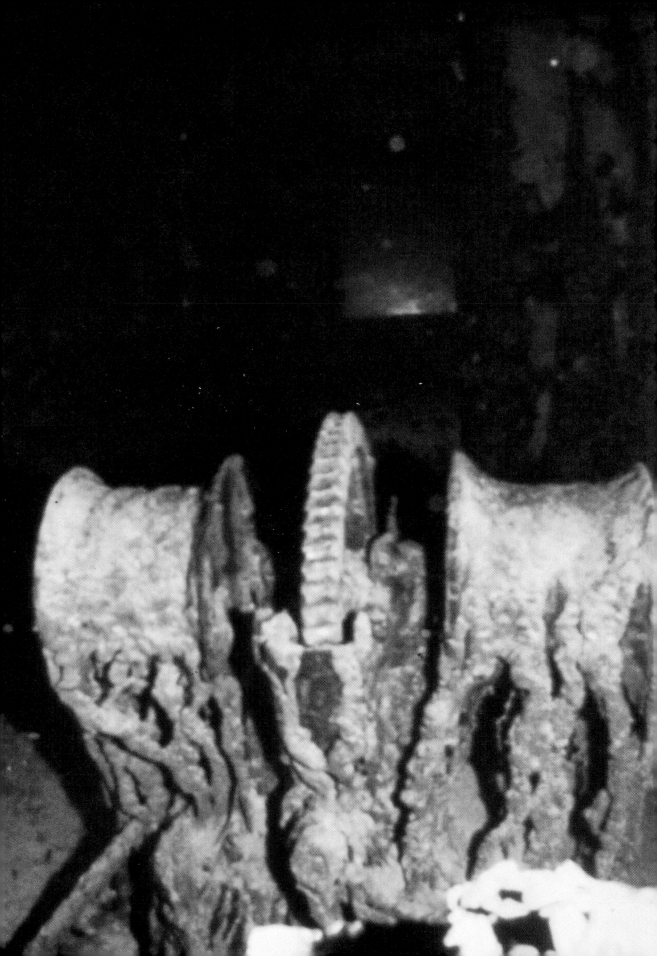

An electric winch on the boatdeck near the officers' cabin can be clearly seen in this picture taken by Jason Jr.

the *Titanic* since it sank. Ballard was in his bunk reading the autobiography of Chuck Yeager, the first man to fly faster than sound. In the control room, Bill Lange and Stu Harris watched miles and miles of endless mud on the TV screens. Suddenly, there it was. Unmistakable wreckage!

"Bingo!" yelled Stu, and for the next several minutes all eyes were glued to the astonishing pictures. Great pieces of the liner came clearly into view. Huge boilers from the ship's deep insides appeared on the TV monitors. Nobody could break themselves away to go fetch Bob Ballard. Finally, the cook was recruited to get him, and for the next hour video tapes were played and replayed.

Far below, across the silent resting place, the tiny Argo plied back and forth just above the field of wreckage. It was approaching 2:20 A.M, almost the exact time of day that the great liner was last seen by human eyes. Without realizing it, the scientists and crew of *Knorr* became aware of what they were watching. At this ship's death, more than 1,500 humans had been lost. Quietly, the scientists gathered on deck and held a small memorial service.

Over the next week Argo and Angus shot thousands of pictures, mapping the debris field and collecting valuable information. The exact spot where the ship lay was precisley mapped at last. It was Labor Day weekend when the *Knorr* sailed for Cape Cod and home. There was much work still to be done, but it would have to wait for another year and another expedition. When they returned, it would be for the most thrilling adventure of all: to land on the deck of the *Titanic* with a submersible carrying two men.

"Rusticles", icicles of rust, nearly cover a porthole of the Titanic in this view taken from Alvin at the bottom of the Atlantic.

Exploring The Wreck

Freed from its cage on Alvin, Jason Jr slowly maneuvers to set down on the deck of the Titanic.

Robert Ballard went back to the *Titanic* in 1986. This time he had bigger and better equipment and a new ship called *Atlantis II*. He was to go down and land on the deck of the *Titanic* with fellow scientist Martin Bowen. They would achieve that incredible feat inside Alvin the submersible. Attached to Alvin was Jason Junior, or JJ, as it came to be called. JJ would be controlled by the two men inside Alvin and it would have special lights, a video camera, and a still camera. Special controls allowed its movement under water to be controlled very precisely. Attached by a line to Alvin, JJ would be the probing eyes exploring *Titanic*.

For twelve days in July 1986, Ballard's team surveyed the great liner. On the first dive they found it difficult to find the ship. In the murky water more than two miles down, a few feet can make all the difference in seeing something or missing it. Just short of giving up, Ballard thought he saw a black mass. They edged Alvin toward it. Suddenly, they faced a sight unlike anything seen on the sea floor before. A giant wall of steel rose straight up from the mud. The *Titanic*!

This picture was taken by Jason Jr flying down the side of the Titanic while Alvin is parked above on the boatdeck.

On the second dive, the view was just as spectacular. Alvin silently drifted across the knife-edge bow of the huge ship, firmly

27

stuck in the silt. Nobody could possibly get it out. The ship was stuck there forever. That pleased Ballard. He feared treasure hunters would try to bring it up. Now he knew they could not. There was quite a lot to recover if anybody wanted some of the ship's belongings, however. Soon the team was working its way across a sea floor littered with debris.

A ghostly doll's head peered up from the mud. A small child had lost it on that terrible night. A wine bottle with its cork still in stood on the bottom. A toilet bowl lay on its side, having torn free as the ship sank. Elsewhere, pots and pans from the kitchens, seats from the first-class lounge, and deck chairs like those last used by Mr. and Mrs. Strauss were found all over the sea floor.

When it sank, the bow of the *Titanic* broke off from the stern about 470 feet back. The stern came to rest 1,970 feet from the bow. Between the two halves of the ship, the floor of the Atlantic was covered with all manner of things from machinery to personal belongings. A safe was discovered, apparently still shut. When special arms on Alvin were used to try to lift it, the back fell out. In all, the collection of objects was like a snapshot of life three-quarters of century before.

The crew quarters below the forward deck and railings can be clearly seen having survived attack by small living organisms at the bottom of the sea.

On one of the most spectacular dives, JJ was carefully controlled to a journey down the grand staircase. Gone were the beautiful paneled walls, the ornate timber stair treads, and the glittering chandeliers. All that remained was the giant opening where the staircase had once been the centerpiece of the ship's lavish design. From what had then been the ceiling, a single light fitting without its bulb or its globe hung motionless. It was time to leave the *Titanic* for the last time.

What Ballard found in his exploration of the *Titanic* helped people understand why the ship sank the way it did. There was no great gash down the ship's side as most people had believed. Instead, the gashes reported by survivors as they looked down the steep hull were plates bulging out with popped rivets. The shock and vibration of hitting the iceberg had caused the ship's side to buckle, letting in water.

Before he returned to the surface for the last time, Dr. Ballard left a plaque on the sea floor near the stern of the *Titanic* where doomed passengers gathered to sing hymns as she slowly sank. It simply said, "In memory of those souls who perished with the *Titanic*, April 14, 1912."

A cargo crane extends beyond the starboard side hole of the Titanic's stern section in this picture taken from towed camera sled Angus.

Glossary

Bow | The forward part of a ship.

Bulkhead | A wall inside a ship which divides it into separate, watertight compartments.

Displacement | The volume of water displaced by a ship when afloat gives an indication of the ship's size.

Screw | A propeller.

Sonar | A device that uses radio waves to detect submerged objects.

Stern | The rear part of a ship.

Submersible | A small vehicle like a submarine that carries people and equipment underwater.

Index